Spousal Prayer

A Way to Marital Happiness

Deacon James Keating, PhD

THE INSTITUTE FOR PRIESTLY FORMATION
IPF PUBLICATIONS

Dedication

To Marianne, Pink, and Mack

Endorsements

"If couples read this book, they will notice that the way of love *is* one. Since God is love, if couples know how to communicate genuine love to one another, they will already know how to be intimate with God. Through three simple principles, couples are shown that their sacramental love for one another is precisely what launches them to the highest happiness possible — happiness in God."

– Christopher West, author, *Fill These Hearts: God, Sex, and the Universal Longing*

"Whether you are a lay person or clergy directly involved with Marriage preparation, consider it providential that this book has crossed your path. Give this book the time it deserves so that you might receive, pray, and be changed in your understanding of the vocation of Marriage!"

– Valerie Conzett, D.Min., L.P.C., Director, Family Life Office, Archdiocese of Omaha, NE

NIHIL OBSTAT: Father Matthew J. Gutowski, STL

IMPRIMATUR: Most Reverend George J. Lucas
Archbishop of Omaha, Neb.
January 18, 2013

THE INSTITUTE FOR PRIESTLY FORMATION
IPF PUBLICATIONS
2500 California Plaza
Omaha, NE
www.priestlyformation.org

Printed in the United States of America
ISBN-13: 978-0-9843792-8-6
ISBN-10: 0-9843792-8-2

Book design by FAITH Catholic Publishing and Communications, Lansing, Mich.

The Institute for Priestly Formation

Mission Statement

The Institute for Priestly Formation was founded to assist bishops in the spiritual formation of diocesan seminarians and priests in the Roman Catholic Church. The Institute responds to the need to foster spiritual formation as the integrating and governing principle of all aspects for priestly formation. Inspired by the biblical-evangelical spirituality of Ignatius Loyola, this spiritual formation has as its goal the cultivation of a deep interior communion with Christ; from such communion, the priest shares in Christ's own pastoral charity. In carrying out its mission, the Institute directly serves diocesan seminarians and priests, as well as those who are responsible for diocesan priestly formation.

The Institute for Priestly Formation
Creighton University
2500 California Plaza
Omaha, NE 68178
www.priestlyformation.org
ipf@creighton.edu

Table of Contents

Introduction[1]

During a marriage preparation session, I once asked a couple if they prayed together. They looked at me blankly for a bit and then said, "We both go to Mass." Worshipping at Mass is the highest form of prayer since, during this worship, we are taken up into Christ's own self offering to the Father out of love for His Bride, the Church. That certainly is praying together. But I was asking something else; I was wondering if they prayed together outside of Mass due to a personal devotion to God. They answered that they did not. We then talked about their earliest memories of prayer as children. The woman remembered saying Grace before meals, and the man recalled being blessed by his mom before he went to bed.

This level of spirituality is fairly common in Catholic families; the family goes to Mass on Sunday, but then Jesus is never really spoken to or listened to again until the next Sunday Mass. When we live this kind of spiritual life, something dangerous happens: We begin to think God is not accessible in the ordinariness of our days, and so we do not develop an ongoing relationship with Him. Inevitably, Sunday Mass can begin to feel boring, or we can feel distant from God during Mass. This reaction is understandable because if we do not have a "daily" relationship with God, then going to Mass becomes like visiting a distant cousin or even a stranger … we share nothing in common. Another reason we might experience this feeling of being distant from God is that we do not know how to really share our hearts with Him, either at Mass or in the course of our daily lives.

The sharing of hearts is a necessary commitment in both marriage and prayer. If we can learn what the key elements to sharing the heart are and equally what the key elements to receiving the heart of another are, then we will know the greatest of intimacy in both prayer and marriage. The mingling of the love of spouse with and in the love of God is — and always has been — the foundation for a life of peace, creativity, and vibrancy, not to mention sanctity. In fact, we cannot even understand what marriage is unless we look at how Christ loved His Bride, the Church, till the end **(Jn 13:1)**. For the baptized, Christ has joined His love for the Church to the Sacrament of Marriage and Marriage, to His love for the Church.

Each couple is called to allow Jesus to bring them into this great love of His. The couple is not supposed to do all the "work" of love; they are called to let Jesus gift them with His own spousal love. In other words, couples should let Jesus live His spousal love for the Church over again in their own love for one another. They do this by simply asking Him in prayer to do so and by sharing their needs and desires with Him. Marriage is *not* a "self-help" relationship; it is a deep partnership with Christ. He shares His life with the couple in the grace of the Sacrament that was given to them on their wedding and continues to pour forth from Christ's heart for them even now. When the couple receives Holy Communion, especially, they should pray, "Lord, live Your spousal love for the Church over again in me. Help me to love my spouse like You love the Church. Love my spouse *for me* and *with me*, Lord. Only You, who are love itself, can empower and support my love for my spouse."

chapter 1

Becoming One

"Ultimately, God wants you to fall in love with your spouse in the manner that **He loves you***: out of sheer gift and in wonder over the beauty of who you are."*

Presentation of the Virgin at the Temple by Domenico Ghirlandaio

Communion with spouse: How do spouses become one?

Ultimately, God wants you to fall in love with your spouse in the manner that He loves you: out of sheer gift and in wonder over the beauty of who you are. Since the male-female relationship is so damaged today (through fornication, cohabitation, divorce and re-marriage, pornography, etc.), cynicism toward love and falling in love rules the day. Many people then come to marriage carrying some emotional injury from past relationships. People in pain are not free to truly give themselves to their beloved. Their marriage preparation *requires healing aimed at emotional and moral freedom.* If such pain is present in you, then Christ is asking that you surrender to Him and let Him stay *with* you and *in* you in order to offer such healing. To suffer the healing of past emotional injuries is necessary so that, on your wedding day, you are free to say "Yes" to love and are not bound to past emotional memories (possessive parents, loneliness, fear of abandonment, promiscuity, pornography, etc.). Let Christ work at the site of this pain. Do not turn away from Him, but bring the pain to Him in prayer and to those to whom your marriage preparation is entrusted, especially your pastor.

For you to be happily married, Christ has to heal you so you can be free to give yourself as a gift to your spouse. In fact, to be someone's spouse, in the Christian sense, is to knowingly enter communion with another to assist in their growth in holiness and moral healing. Keeping your vows of fidelity until death and possessing openness of heart to give and receive love creates the most secure arena for spiritual and emotional healing. This remedy can occur because spouses are willing to say one simple sentence, "I am not going anywhere," and then back up this statement with one simple promise to "remain" vowed to the one they love. This is the surest sign that spouses understand both the attraction of love ("I desire you and you alone") and the work of love ("I will suffer my and your needed healing/conversion"). To "suffer" the healing of your spouse is to endure his or her spiritual, moral, and emotional conversion by way of your graced and promised vowed love. The spiritual goal of Catholic marriage is to mediate grace from God for the mutual conversion of spouses. The vow is, "I am not going anywhere." With this vow, and with God's help, one spouse sees the other spouse through his or her moral and emotional conversion. This vow frees the spouses to live in truth and communicate their struggles with each other. The vow for spouses to stay faithful until death gives each partner the courage to receive the truth about his or her present weaknesses and faults without the thought that, "I will be abandoned"**(Jn 14:18)**.

Most people come into a marriage emotionally, spiritually, or morally disadvantaged to a greater or lesser extent. Since this is the case, each spouse may or may not be able to attend to the pain of their spouse as they are coping with the effects of their own distress. To counteract this state of mutual strain and, therefore, mutual unavailability to one another, it is good for couples to get outside help with their needed healings and, most especially, to seek freedom from these difficulties during the marriage preparation period.

To vow to remain ("Whoever remains in me and I in him will bear much fruit." **Jn 15:5**) with your spouse until death and then to entrust your heart to, and share your prayers with, him or her creates the emotional and spiritual *security* necessary for a person to entrust their body to their spouse. You will respect the body of your spouse if you do one thing: "clothe" that body, not with fabric, but with true and lasting *intimacy*.[2] Mature communion between spouses depends upon emotional, spiritual, and physical safety. "I will reveal all only if I am assured you will receive all and not run from me." In creating such a safe place called marriage, a man and a woman know happiness. Anything less than this kind of safety carries the *potential* for such happiness, but not yet its fullness.

Marital intimacy, then, is the real sharing of the heart and body within the safety and trust of a prayerful and vowed relationship until death. This intimacy is the glue that holds a relationship together. Without such intimacy, outside forces can interfere with the commitment and seduce a spouse to look for emotional safety elsewhere, in places where self-donation and revelation will not be secure but, perhaps, only temporarily received (sexual affairs, emotional affairs, immature and lingering emotional dependency upon one's family of origin, etc.). In this temporary "intimacy," a spouse may receive false consolation, mistaking it for vowed security. Much pain is caused by couples who do not bestow intimacy as their primary gift to one another. Intimacy is demanded by the human heart and, when real, is its deepest place of rest; when received within a communion of prayer, it becomes the deepest place of life's meaning.

To love is to give the self for the good of your beloved. This giving, however, is not simply a series of discreet acts of service for your spouse. Love also involves the desire to abide in the presence of another. To be in your spouse's presence physically does not mean, however, that you have achieved union with him or her. Union involves not only service, not only sexual intercourse, but, perhaps most especially, the commitment to reveal the heart, to reveal thoughts, feelings, and desires. These heart movements are not revealed in service of the self. In other words, they are not revealed to relieve oneself of an affective burden ("I am angry; I will tell you about it so I feel better"). No, these heart movements are shared because you have come to know that *your spouse will receive these interior movements as a sure path to union* ("I am angry so I will tell you about it to guard our communion. I do not want this anger to separate us in any way"). Without such deep sharing, a couple may simply co-exist in a house, efficiently choosing the most amenable route to accomplishing daily duties, but, in reality, missing one another, never really being in the real presence of the other. To live in the real presence of your spouse, you need to commit to reveal your heart and to receive your spouse's heart, thus achieving intimacy.

The best way to achieve intimacy is intentionally to commit yourself to a few vital actions. First, regularly behold your spouse. Second, daily, in a relaxed atmosphere, choose to listen to your spouse. Third, forgive your spouse and incorporate into your love any hurt he or she has caused. Finally, love one another within an atmosphere of prayer, letting prayer be the oxygen of your marriage.

Beholding Your Spouse

To behold your spouse does not mean that you stare at him or her with your eyes fixed upon his or her face. To behold means that you allow your spouse's heart, your spouse's identity, to be received at the deepest level of your being. To behold your spouse means that you have allowed your spouse's presence to affect you, move you, and awaken you to love. Beholding has something to do with seeing, of course; one does look at his or her spouse and, in looking, "sees" the beauty there. There is more to beholding than looking, however. Beholding is brought to its proper end when your spouse, whose beauty you see with your eyes, now becomes the beauty whom you carry in your heart. The way your spouse enters your heart and abides there is through an opening in your own heart which sensitizes you to, and makes you attentive to, his or her presence. This opening in your own heart is a "wound" that only your spouse can cause; it is an ache to receive love, as well as give it. This wound is near the core of what it means to be a human being created in the image of God.

The wound is not a pain in a negative sense, but a pain or a suffering in a positive sense. A positive wound, in the situation of marriage, is one that is "given" when the spouse beholds the beauty of his or her beloved. When I say "wound," I am saying that your spouse has affected you deeply, changed you for the better by virtue of who he or she is. He or she has made the deepest *impression* upon you.

Giving the self and receiving the spouse is the rhythm that heals the disordered attention to the self or the hate of self that lies ready to pounce at the smallest suffering or fear. This disorder is always saying; "What about me?" or "Who will think of me?" or "I am worthless; I am not worthy of love."

The more you choose to be in the presence of your spouse, however, the more deeply the spouse enters the heart so that fears are diminished. To be in your spouse's presence does not mean you give up all commitments that take you from one another physically; that would be an impossible life. To live in one's presence does, in fact, demand a commitment to be together physically; but what is most vital is that when you *are* together in the same space, you suffer your spouse's presence as a chosen gift. To suffer the presence of the spouse is to make choices that deflate your own ego and, instead, carry consoling assurances to your spouse. To console your spouse, you choose to see his or her beauty and allow this beauty to displace your ego. This displacing of the ego is not easy; that is why marriage is a suffering. What is easy is to remain in our own presence. What is life-altering and healing is to suffer the coming of another into the space formally filled by the ego. If you suffer this coming, you will eventually enjoy marriage, and your spouse's presence. If you keep resisting the death of your ego, or the healing of self-hate, then your situation is clear; your spouse, his presence and his needs, will be seen as a threat, a person who wants only to "take" from you … time, desires, vacation choices, weekend preoccupations, etc. Or, in the case of the one who suffers from self-hate, she suffers the inability to receive the love of her spouse. "My self-hate pushes away the healing of being loved." In Christ, we can suffer the death of the ego and learn to receive the love of another. To go through this suffering with Christ can end our "self-made loneliness" in and through His power of love. He will not abandon you. He remains always to complete your joy.

So, can we look again at our spouse and see what we have, perhaps, forgotten or never fully received? He or she is a beautiful creation of God and a gift to us. Of course, this beauty is difficult to see at all times and in all circumstances; but since *marriage is being given to us* in grace at every moment *from the Bridegroom* Himself (that is why it is a Sacrament), there is always hope that intimacy can define one's relationship. The cancellation of that hope — on our side, never on God's — is assured if we refuse to turn to Christ and each other for the strength to suffer the *death of our own ego* or if we refuse to receive love and, in doing so, *let self-hate remain*.

Listening to Your Spouse

A second vital component for achieving spousal intimacy is for both of you to become authentic listeners. The first listening is not really done with the ears, but with the love-soaked mind and heart given to you at Baptism. You behold your spouse in Christ and hear Christ say: "This spouse of yours is really mine; he will always be mine, but because my love is overflowing in generosity, I share my joy with you." The joy of marriage is found in the sharing of love with one another as Christ is loving your spouse through you and you, through your spouse. The joy is being caught up in this dynamic of mutual love which always yields a deep peace, a peace given from God. Christ further says, "Take good care of your spouse for he is meant to live with Me in heaven. His relationship with Me is in his hands, but I have given you to him so that you can help him reach holiness. Use every grace that marriage gives you to assist Me in welcoming him into eternity." Now, that voice of Christ is something you can hear only with the *ears of faith*. If you do not hear that encouragement from Christ to help your spouse to heaven, whatever else you hear with your ears *may be off-key*. The mutual sanctity of the spouses, as well as the raising of children, is the point of sacramental marriage. When we move from *beholding* our spouse to *listening* to our spouse, we do not want to forget what we are listening for at the deepest level: Is my spouse, in her actions, dispositions, and commitments, living in Christ?

The more common level of listening is well-known to any spouse; it is simply the commitment to pay attention to your spouse's words and the disposition of their heart from which these words are born. The reason this common level of listening is so well-known is because we so often experience our frustration in failing to attain it! The universal difficulty in marriage is to stay on the task of paying attention to our spouse. There are many reasons for failing to listen, but most come down to selfishness, thoughtlessness, and laziness. After a while, couples take each other's presence for granted; that is why listening has to become a virtue and not simply an act that is occasionally exercised. As with the practice of any virtue, in the beginning, it is more about willing it than loving it. However, married couples have the advantage of actually liking one another and desiring one another in companionship. That should make it easy to listen to one another, yes? Well, yes and no. The lifelong commitment of marriage can actually undermine the choice to pay attention to your spouse: "He will be around later; I will pay attention then." The actual knowledge we hold that our spouse will be with us "until death do us part" may unwittingly play a role in taking our spouse for granted. This attitude must be resisted.

To reject this temptation to take your spouse for granted, remember the first reality that listening is built upon: beholding your spouse. We want to behold our spouse, receive him or her as the gift he or she is, and then, in gratitude, begin to focus upon our spouse's words as he or she speaks. This is not to be some formal action as if we have to methodically stop, look, and listen! Remember that, over time, your spouse enters and lives in your heart. After many years of your choosing her welfare, she is internalized; you come to hold her in your being. This beholding and listening to your spouse becomes second nature, but we need to remember that choosing to cherish the one you live with for many decades can wax and wane. That being noted, there will be times when you do have to formally stop your drifting and distracted mind and hear your heart speak, "Wait a minute; that is Helen. I love her; I choose her; I will listen to her."

To master the art and gift of listening to your spouse is truly a vital virtue, a virtue that over many decades of marriage will secure your bond with her or him and bring joy to your heart as you truly experience authentic affective union. So, our listening is founded upon our capacity to behold; and then, in the integration of these two attitudes, we become more capable of the third reality upon which intimacy is built: forgiveness.

Forgiving Your Spouse

If we do not master the virtues of beholding our spouse gratefully and then listening to his or her heart and voice, then, in due time, we will fall into some form of alienation from one another. As a result, forgiveness will have to be offered to restore the union. To forgive your spouse for not paying attention to you is to recognize that such behavior is a threat to intimacy. Intimacy is living in the habit of a mature truthful exchange of the affective movements of one's heart. Intimacy is a form of communion that comes about as a result of a spouse offering himself as a gift to his beloved in a reciprocal exchange. When intimacy is undermined, the communion lost by neglect of the spouse has to be regained. This process of regaining intimacy by way of forgiveness can be painful since it involves receiving into your heart the very one who hurt you. It is a kind of "love of enemy" that Christ bid us to embrace (**Mt 5:44**). At the time of the spousal neglect, your spouse was, in a sense, your "enemy"; she placed her interests against the interests of the marriage bond. She chose "I" instead of "we." In so doing, she caused you unjust pain.[3] But this pain should not define your marriage. It is the reality of the vows *that defines your marriage*, always the hope of the "Yes" that is embodied in the lifelong commitment; and, ultimately, it is always the fidelity of Christ, the faithful One, Who lives within you Who defines your marriage.

When forgiveness is necessary, it is vital to call upon Christ and allow Him to gift you with the grace to incorporate the harm you suffered from your spouse into your love for him or her. These places of pain, then, actually become meeting places between you and Christ because only by His power can you forgive your spouse. Whether the offense inflicted by your spouse is great (infidelity) or small (forgot a personally important event or date), Christ wants to be the agent for reconciliation between the two of you. Christ wants you to call upon Him and allow His Spirit to work at the site of the pain in order to fuse more securely the bond between you and your spouse. If we do not turn our sorrow over to Christ, we risk the possibility that the suffering inflicted by our spouse will define the marriage. When that happens, you begin to think out of the pain and decide out of the pain; and, thus, the pain becomes your new identity. The pain can replace your real vocation as spouse and become a "vocation" of habit. When you invite Christ into the suffering that healing demands, then these wounds no longer define you; instead, *Christ's actions to heal the suffering and lead you to forgiveness for the sake of the marriage define you.* To have your life defined by Christ's power to heal gives you deep peace. This peace is born of your inviting Christ to be active in your healing. To invite Him to be so active is simply to live out what you chose to become when you surrendered to one another in the vows — married in the Lord.

When you ask Christ to heal a spouse-inflicted wound, I invite you to consider the following actions:

1. ***Acknowledge the wound to your spouse.*** Allow your spouse to admit guilt and sorrow, and receive this grief into your heart as a sign of his or her love for you. Assure your spouse of your forgiveness of him or her. If it takes time to offer this forgiveness, that is fine; simply say to your spouse that you are open to forgiving, but that the pain is too recent, and you are still experiencing it. What happens if your spouse refuses to admit his or her guilt? If your spouse refuses to admit his or her guilt for intentionally harming you, then perhaps you may choose to do the following: Invite your spouse to consider the pain you are in. In private, pray and fast for your spouse to be converted; offer your participation in the Eucharist for him or her, and approach your spouse again, asking if he or she would like forgiveness. If the injuries continue without repentance on his or her part, consult a priest and a therapist for further help.

There is an added reality to consider, as well. What *is God doing* in you and in your spouse when he or she refuses to admit guilt? First, He is asking that you trust *Him* more deeply. In the midst of the pain caused by your spouse and the further pain delivered by his or her refusal to admit responsibility for the injury,

Christ is actively inviting you to rest in Him, find healing in Him. Christ wants your prayer to go deeper now and for you to spend more time with Him in your sorrow and pain and anger. He wants to join you in this difficult situation to love you within it. He, too, knew such sorrow in the rejection by those who killed Him and in their unrepentant attitudes even after much wrong was committed against Him in mocking, scourging, humiliations, and, finally, His unthinkable murder. At any one point, His persecutors could have come to their senses, stopped, and repented; and He would have forgiven them. They, however, went their own way **(Acts 1:25)**. Right now, your spouse is going his or her *own* way … but you are *not* alone. Christ is one with *you*.

Secondly, what is God doing in your unrepentant spouse? His Spirit is loving your spouse; and, hopefully, your spouse will respond as he or she listens to the conscience, the place where all decisions that honor truth and love are made. As acts of love joined to the power of God's love, your prayers, fasting, and Eucharistic worship work to hasten the day of repentance in your spouse. If your spouse refuses to repent even after your prayers, fasting, and adoration are complete, these will have deeply affected *your own intimacy with God*. It will *not* be your fault if no sign of regret is ever offered to you. Lack of sorrow in your spouse is *not* the result of you not praying *hard* enough, or fasting *long* enough. No, you are loving him or her to the best of your ability, and your love and Christ's love are combining to bring light to your spouse. It is your spouse's heart that bears the responsibility if he or she stays separated from the need to repent, not yours.

2. ***Bring the emotional effects of the wound and the wound itself to Christ in prayer.*** Show Him the wound. Offer it to Him; show Him the pain so He can enter it and love you from *within it*, "See, Lord, my pain (name the pain)." There is no need to speak

a lot about the pain to Christ; just keep holding the wound open before Him so He can pour His mercy and love into it.

3. ***It is best to do this "showing" while holding a Crucifix, while in adoration before the Blessed Sacrament, or while reading an appropriate Scripture verse.*** Do not minimize the wound or excuse the behavior of your spouse; what you offer to Christ must be the *real* wound and the real pain if He is going to heal it. God lives in reality, and so must we, if we are to have communion with God.

4. ***Continue to bring this wound to the Lord for as long as it takes to incorporate it into your love for your spouse.*** We always will bear the scars of the wounds caused by our spouse, but the wounds do not guide our relationship with him or her; we let the forgiveness that Christ gifts us with guide our marriage. Healing is especially secured through the Sacrament of Reconciliation and when we contemplatively receive Holy Communion at Mass. To receive Holy Communion contemplatively means that we enter into deep conversation with Christ, who is now in us, about all the wounds we carry. The Eucharist's whole purpose is to bring about healing.[4] The assistance of a good spiritual director is also suggested, especially if the wound is deep, indicating a deep prayer life is needed by the wounded spouse in order to forgive.[5]

Praying With and For Your Spouse

Beholding, listening, and forgiving your spouse are essential prerequisites for praying with your spouse since prayer is *the most intimate experience* a couple can share and, thus, *demands the deepest level of trust.* Prayer is such an experience because, by its nature, it brings a couple to the very source of their love, the outpouring life and beauty of the Trinity itself. All love is from, and abides in, God. To become vulnerable to being loved by

God, receiving His love as the very life breath of one's marriage, requires a trust that may, at first, seem too much to risk. If we think about our lives of faith for a moment, this fear dissipates. Those of you who received the gift of faith from your parents as children, you have been praying and opening your hearts to God at some level ever since you can remember. In this way, you have a history of prayer. When you marry, you simply want to invite your spouse into the stream of that history. Of course, your prayer life needs to mature, and you are not a child anymore. Start your shared prayer life, however, from within the familiarity of whatever your parents may have gifted you with: Bible verses, the Rosary, Sunday Mass, Adoration of the Blessed Sacrament, meditation or the noticing of God in everyday life and nature, and so on. Remember, also, that you have been learning to trust one another since you first began to date and now into your engagement or marriage. For years, you may have been beholding the beauty of your beloved, listening to him or her, and forgiving the weaknesses he or she possesses or inflicts upon you. Here, you see that marriage simply deepens a history of intimacy that you have already been living, no matter the level or how tentatively you began your intimacy.

So, you are not beginning at zero; you have a history with God and a history with your beloved. Now, invite one another into that history more regularly, more deeply.

On to prayer. What is prayer? Prayer is a pure receptivity, as Pope Benedict XVI has taught. Prayer is our openness to be loved by God in our present state. "In our present state" is vital to accept because some people feel they can go to God to receive His love only if they are feeling good or pure or in a positive frame of mind. God wants us to come to Him and receive His love no matter our subjective state before Him. In fact, our spiritual growth demands that we go to Him particularly when we are feeling bad; in that condition, we are most susceptible to temptation, most eager to seek artificial consolation from sin. "Master, to whom shall we go? You have the words of eternal life" (**Jn 6:68**). That is what the Apostle said, and his question is ours. And the answer is clear that we are to go to God when temptations or difficulties arise.

When you pray, either in good times or bad, you allow your heart to be seen and known by God's love. The most vital aspect of prayer is *to receive His love*. Marital prayer is a receiving of the life of God that we are called to communicate to our spouse. Prayer is a *grace* (which means the gift of God sharing His life and love with us) and, therefore, we are called to ask the Holy Spirit to help us with prayer. He will help us with great joy and eagerness because the Holy Spirit is the love between God the Father and God the Son, a love so real, beautiful, and eternal that it is one of the Persons of the Holy Trinity. To want to pray is to tap into the joy of God whose sole essence is to love. This love is so powerful that it took on flesh and became a human being. God gifted us with Jesus so that the Trinity's love could reach us in the deepest aspects of our human sufferings and joys. Since Christ took on flesh, no one can say, "God does not understand my pain or share in my joy." *All that is human is joined to God in Christ.*

It is prayer that facilitates the Spirit of Christ to reach your deepest suffering and deepest joy. Prayer is powerful because it gives permission to God to affect your heart and mind and will. In prayer, you want God to "permeate" you; and if you let Him permeate your being, you will see how prayer moves from being simply your words spoken on your lips to His Word speaking within your heart.[6] The goal is to become a prayerful person, a prayerful couple, to have God dwell in your being, you and Him breathing together. God wants to labor within you to achieve this goal.

chapter 2

Praying more deeply

> *"**Praying** can be intimidating for the same reasons that falling in love can be: to do so brings us to the **core** meaning of **human life**."*

Annunciation by Fra Angelico

Communion with God: How do we pray more deeply?

Praying can be intimidating for the same reasons that falling in love can be: to do so brings us to the core meaning of human life. Why would coming close to the actual meaning of life be intimidating? Both prayer and falling in love move us from one set of attachments to another, attachments that secure our human dignity, not those which undermine it. The resistance to falling in love and to praying is the resistance to let go of artificially consoling attachments. In the case of marriage, the artificial consolation would be the "single life" where all options are left open. In the case of prayer, the artificial consolation would be the choice to remain wedded to the culture of distraction, entertainment, and escape. Both prayer and love bring us into reality … our sinful nature resists reality and prefers a world of *our own making*.

So, when first approaching a new commitment to prayer, expect it to be a struggle. Struggle will not define the entire history of your prayer life, but struggle will be present because the temptation to live in a world of your own making and not the real world will come roaring back over time. Temptation to give up on the real world and head back to the culture of delayed maturity will, at times, overwhelm our desire to pray. When this occurs, do not grow angry or disappointed with yourself. Failure in prayer is to be *expected* and welcomed: expected because we grow weary of doing good, and *welcomed* because failure proves our poverty before good intentions. If we taste the failure as an encounter with our poverty and weakness, a door will open offering true conversion. By poverty, I mean our experience of trying to accomplish "success" in our spiritual lives and then realizing that the spiritual life is not something that we create, achieve, or win. The spiritual is given when we come before

God with a true and real disposition: "without [God] you can do nothing" (Jn 15:5). This conversion, making a turn to *depend totally upon God and surrender to His power,* is truly the beginning of real prayer. Until we admit we cannot pray, admit we are in need of Divine help, our prayer will last only as long as our willpower. Instead, we are to admit our powerlessness to pray and receive it as a gift that we ask for always (1 Thes 5:17).

Another vital point before we begin a life of marital prayer is to remember that God loves your spouse in his or her unique personality. Marriage makes us one, but we can become one only because we are singular persons. "Precisely through being man and woman, each of them is given to the other as a unique and unrepeatable subject, as 'I', as person."[7] We are to retain that singularity toward one another. God loves your spouse as "other," not as Himself; and so you should love your spouse, as well, as "other," not as yourself. Now, of course, we do achieve and are gifted with union over the time of our intimacy, but true love never effects a merger of identities or the loss of personality. In fact, the more I receive the love of God and the love of my spouse and love them in return, the more I become my real self. Nothing of me is lost in giving; the self is found in giving to another (Jn 12:24).

God will come to your spouse and to you in your unique personalities. Initially, this can cause difficulties in trying to pray together as a couple. Perhaps your wife likes silence, and you like to read the Bible out loud; or she likes the Rosary, and you like Eucharistic Adoration. One of you may like to pray as a couple only with the children present while your spouse wants to pray with the children and then later on in the day, with you alone … and so on. Compromises will be necessary in most cases if a couple is going to commit some time to common prayer. Try to begin praying by agreeing on a method that may not be your "favorite," but one that still has an attraction for you. The attraction could simply be that you *want to pray* with the spouse no matter what method he or she chooses. A key truth about prayer is to remember that prayer is a relationship, *not* a technique. As Sister Ruth Burrows, Carmelite teacher of prayer, has noted, in beginning to pray there is no problem to overcome, nothing to master, nothing to "learn" or become "skilled" in.[8] There is simply a devastating question that stands before us when we begin to pray: "Do I want to be with God or not?" In this question, the nuptial meaning of God's relationship to us becomes clear: all God wants is us. Do we want God?

In a holy relationship, the spouses desire one another; they want to be together and, in so doing, draw their joy and life from the mutual exchange of one another as gift. In prayer, the one who prays desires to be with God; that is the key to all Christian living: Do you desire God? God has already given His body as gift in Jesus Christ's life. Your entire marriage and your prayer life is a response to this gift of God's. Both your marriage and your faith involve the same movement: the beholding of beauty in both your spouse and God and your surrender in trust to this beauty, this radiance of Truth that attracts you and holds you "until death do you part."

What is the beauty of God in Christ that attracts us? It is not His words, per se, or His physical appearance. It is His *action*. Christ is beautiful because He *chooses* God the Father and the needs of others over Himself. He *gives* Himself for the sake of others. He *donates* His entire person in the service of healing others. Since we are made in God's image, we are called by the Church to live like Christ by having Him live in us. "Man, who is the only creature on earth which God willed for itself, *cannot fully find himself except through a sincere gift of himself.*"[9] There is nothing more beautiful than this because such action is the very expression of the truth of who God is: God is love. God, therefore, is beauty itself, and our attraction to beauty indicates why we were created — to be with Him. Our restless search for beauty, as it is God Himself, hints at its awesome power — *to redeem us from sin.*

Here are three ways to behold this divine beauty more deeply in prayer:

1. ***Ask for the gift to want to be with God.*** Since sin is such a large part of our human experience, it is not "natural" to want God. We are born simply wanting to please and think about the self. Ask God, therefore, to deepen your awareness of His presence and His Beauty; ask Him to show you "His face" so that you might desire Him most of all. Ask Him to place a desire for Him in your heart through grace **(Jn 7:37f)**. Asking God for this desire is most important for prayer because we cannot assume we will "want" to be with God. Even Christ Himself encouraged us to ask for healing and His presence **(Mk 10:51)**.

2. ***Ask for the gift to suffer the coming of Christ into your heart so He might move you away from those disordered attachments that give you more pleasure than being with God.*** Pray for the gift *of suffering* the coming of Christ because detachment is excruciating, even with God's grace. We love pleasure more than God. Now, at times, the effect of love is pleasure, so pleasure is not intrinsically evil; but it can be evil, if chosen for itself. To choose pleasurable things for themselves is dangerous **(Mt 19:24)** and may keep you from moving toward God. Choosing disordered attachments (sins) keeps the ego in charge and feeds it the distractions it craves — distractions that keep you enslaved to them. Some of these attachments are well-known to us: pride, sloth, anger, lust, gluttony, envy, greed. We also are attached to activities like excessive entertainment, concern about our physical appearance, disproportionate use of the Internet, computer, social media, television, and so on.

If you are to avoid sinful attachments, you must remember that the core of life is not you but Another. If you stay in a world of distracting pleasures and entertainment, you will not progress in intimacy with God and, therefore, will not progress in freedom. To be free is to be available to receive God's love unobstructed by serious sin or habits of self-centeredness. The opposite of freedom is sin.

To be free is to be with Him and in Him. To be free is *to be bound to Him* in a communion of love, in a reciprocal sharing of the self as gift. Before we reach this life of communion, we are either moving toward such communion or away from it. Spiritual and moral freedom demands that we be bound to God; our culture demands that we be ready to break all promises for the sake of personal pleasure. We have to choose to whom or to what we will become *freely bound*. That is the drama of our lives.

3. *Ask the Spirit to pray in your heart.* Begin your prayer by inviting the Spirit to pray in you, to bring you to the Father and bind you to Jesus. Remember: your prayer is mostly the work of God in you; your work is to allow Him to reveal your sins, your self-defeating attachments, and to receive His love. Once you make yourself available to God in this way, He initiates your communion with Him to occur, healing to be accomplished, and freedom to be restored. Remember that you are poor **(Rom 8:26)**; you need Him to bring you to Himself. And so, pray, "Come, Holy Spirit." We are told in the Bible to "pray without ceasing" **(1 Thes 5:17)**. You cannot do such a thing since you are so weak, but you can give your soul to the Spirit *who will be the very means of communication between yourself and God. To give your soul to the Holy Spirit is to give your soul to love. In such a giving, your capacity to pray will increase.*

The Holy Spirit's name, the Advocate **(Jn 14:16)**, literally means "one who is called alongside of another in order to assist." The Holy Spirit, who is the love between the Father and the Son, dwells within our hearts, and there, He prays for us, with us (**Rom 8:26-28**). Surrender to His presence within your heart, and ask Him to pray *in you*. When you are weak, tired, frustrated, frightened, just yield to Him, and let Him pray in you.

And so, as a married couple, you want to ask for the desire to pray, the courage for the grace of conversion, and the insight to know that prayer is more a gift of the indwelling Spirit than a task you accomplish. In what concrete ways ought your prayer proceed?

Behold

Earlier, this book advised that you are to behold your spouse so that his or her beauty as a person can affect you and change you for the better and establish a deeper union between the two of you. Recall that to behold your spouse means you allow his or her heart, your spouse's identity, to be received at the deepest level of your being. To behold your spouse means that you have allowed his or her presence to affect you, move you, and awaken you to love. Beholding is brought to its proper end when your spouse, whose beauty you see with your eyes, now becomes the beauty whom you carry in your heart. How, then, do we behold God in prayer? First, know that your spouse is an icon of Christ for you. Christ reaches you through your spouse, and you reach Christ through your love of your spouse, as well. Marriage is a Sacrament because the love between you and your spouse is a "place" to receive and be received by God. So, first, realize in faith that, when you behold your spouse, you are beholding Christ. Your entire married life, then, is potentially a prayer as your consciousness deepens to accept this mystery of Christ's presence already in your spouse's love for you and yours for him or her.

Beyond this presence of Christ in one another, how else can you behold Christ in your prayer as a couple? First, before you pray, retrieve a Crucifix or a piece of art that depicts Jesus in some fashion. Place this in your hands or on a table before the two of you. Ask for the Holy Spirit to lead you into prayer, and then simply gaze upon the depiction of Christ in silence. Let the image move you to speak to Him in some way about what is foremost in your heart. If you choose to hold the image, place it in your hands or hold it against your heart. When you are finished praying, pass the image or Crucifix to your spouse and let him or her enter the silence, as well. In this way, the image helps to focus your minds, alleviates controllable distractions, and places your imaginations in the right frame of mind.

Jesus is real and lives among us. He now lives in us as Spirit and can use images to draw us deeper into communion with Himself. When we behold Jesus in an image, we are not simply gazing at a piece of art and admiring its handiwork. Recall how you behold your spouse. First, you notice his or her physical beauty; but then, you allow this beauty to lead you into your spouse's being, his or her heart. Now, we allow the Spirit to do the same with our prayer life. We gaze upon the image of Christ, or imagine Him as we read one of our favorite Scripture stories, then let the Spirit draw us *through the image to the person* of Christ; and there, we converse with God.

When I say let the Spirit draw you through the image of Christ, I mean that the Spirit will gently move you from the image before you or the Scripture you read, and soon, you will no longer be thinking *about an image or pondering ideas*. You will have been *ushered into a Presence!*

In times of joy or despair, to have an image of Christ nearby is crucial for spiritual growth and consolation. Fill your home with sacred images, and let your eyes rest upon them, receiving the grace of the Spirit as He leads you from image to Person. When the Person of Christ emerges from the image, rest with Him and reveal everything in your heart, just as you would to your spouse. Such personal revelation to the Trinity is the surest route to intimacy with Him.

For newlyweds, imagine how wonderful it is to bring your first baby home and for that baby never to have known any other environment than one filled with sacred images and holy prayer between mom and dad. This is exactly the spiritual oxygen your children need to receive the love of God by way of your own faith, hope, and love. Children want to join the prayer of their mother and father, just like they want to join you when you spontaneously dance together in your home. In such dancing, children normally do not choose to break up mom and dad dancing; they just want to join in. If children are born into a home of a praying couple, they will *want* to join in such activity from the very start. For those already with children, it is *never* too late to start to allow this oxygen of prayer to fill the home.

Listen

Next, we want to listen to Christ. Once we have been drawn into His presence by the power of the Spirit through the image, then we can begin to listen to Him speak. In your conversation with Christ, intimacy is born, sustained, and deepened. This is why conversation with God is so vital to human happiness. When we converse with God, we move toward intimacy with the Trinity — the intimacy we were destined to live within. This intimacy with God is what we are all looking for; but often, we order our desires to other, less dignified, goals. In prayer, as in marriage, we want our desires to lead us to communion with the one we love. We do not want our desires to begin and end in self-gratification.

Listening between husbands and wives is similar to listening to God. Listening can simply be stated as *the commitment to pay attention to your spouse's words and the disposition of his or her heart from which these words are born.* This, too, is the attitude we need to listen to God; pay attention to His Word and His posture toward us. His word is clearly revealed in Scripture, and His posture toward us always is uniform: He is truth itself carried to us in merciful love.

Listening to God from *within our hearts*, however, appears to be the most difficult part of prayer for most people. This is so because we only "hear" our own voice, and we have trouble discerning His voice from ours. We also hear "lies" within our own hearts that are born from our suffering and even demonic influence ("You are no good, not worthy, a failure," and so on). God's voice never attacks your person; He affirms or gently calls you away from immorality, but He never condemns you *as a person.* When you hear that voice, know that it is never God's.

There is a common fear within people who start to pray: "Am I making up all these words in my head? Who is really speaking here, me or God?" Remember that Pope Benedict XVI said prayer was pure receptivity. That means when I pray, I am called to receive a word beyond my own. To receive a word beyond my own is what we welcome when we grasp our own insufficiency. *My* ideas are not enough; I need God to speak and to lead me.

God speaks to us through the ideas we hear in our own minds. He speaks through the feelings we carry in our own hearts. These ideas and feelings have *to be discerned*, but know that God gently uses our own thoughts, fills them with truth, and invites us to pay attention to that truth. Of course, God can inspire a person with visions and locutions (God's audible voice directly received), but these means are not His normal ways of speaking. What is normal in prayer is to hear deep within your heart, "I love you"; "You are mine"; "I forgive you"; "I want to give you this vocation," and so on. He speaks gently, conveying His will through our desires, ideas, attractions, and feelings. Faith, hope, and love keep us in communion with the mystery of God's love in Christ. Embracing these three gifts — faith, hope, and love — is our surest foundation for progress in the spiritual life. We should ask for the grace to have these gifts and virtues activated within us as the glue that holds us fast to God, even when our ideas, feelings, and desires are silent.

One thing is certain in prayer: if you ever hear a voice saying, "You are bad," "You are a failure," "You are not worthy of my love," it is either an unhealed emotional wound speaking from your pain, or Satan attaching himself to such pain in an attempt to drive you to despair. When we despair of living our true identities as sons and daughters of God, then prayer fades and Satan has a victory. Listen only to those voices that bear truth in love and mercy and never to voices that carry condemnation, voices that leave you isolated from Christ's merciful love.

When my ideas, feelings, and desires are active, how, then, do I discern which ones are from God? First, normally any idea that agrees with moral virtue and Catholic teaching can be followed as good and of God. You do not need to go into deep prayer to decide if you should be honest in dealing with your business's finances. Stealing is wrong. If you are attracted to stealing, you know it is a temptation. In the case of stealing, your prayer should be about surrendering to Christ's power to avoid this temptation. Second, when you pray and are not sure whether the thoughts, feelings, or desires are yours or God's, go to your pastor or other competent spiritual leader in the Catholic Church for guidance. Third, we can have sure knowledge about the origins of these thoughts, feelings, and desires by asking three simple questions: Do these affective movements carry joy or peace with them? Do these affective movements deepen my faith, hope, or love? If you can answer "Yes" to these two questions, then presume they may be from God. Finally, do these affective movements leave me feeling "dry" or "heavy" and without attraction to holiness or things of God? If you can answer "Yes," then, initially, presume that these movements or "voices" within your heart *are not from God* and resist them. As previously noted, it is best to have some competent person help you follow only those thoughts, feelings, and desires that deepen faith, hope, and love. Over time and within a true commitment to prayer as a couple, you may begin to function as informal spiritual "guides" for one another. This is one of the great gifts of marriage "in the Lord," as He loves to affirm His truth and His love through the words and attentive presence of your own spouse.

So, to summarize, listening is a crucial aspect of prayer. It includes coming to notice your own thoughts and feelings, embracing the moral teachings of the Catholic Church, which implies embracing a painful moral conversion where needed, distinguishing the "voices" in your heart so that you readily recognize which ones come from the indwelling Holy Spirit and should be followed and which ones come from error, unhealed wounds, or evil spirits and should be resisted. Our main attitude in prayer is to pay attention to God within our hearts.

Along with learning how to listen *within our hearts*, we also can listen to God and remain in His presence by way of experiences from *"outside" our hearts*. Of course, even experiences involving other persons or events have to be processed by our hearts, but such experiences have their origin in others and not within our own thoughts, feelings, or desires. How does this kind of listening occur?

Such experience is already well-known to you. Think of the times when, from afar, you notice your child playing; behold him deeply, and then, in silence, receive him in love all over again. More fascinating is that, at the moment you receive your child more deeply into your heart, you receive your own vocation as mom or dad at a more profound level. The reception of this experience in faith, hope, and love is a form of listening to God. Other examples of listening to God "outside" the heart might be when a neighbor says a "random" comment about his marriage that rivets you upon *your own* marriage and its needed reform, or perhaps you attend an event that leaves you empty emotionally, raising within you a desire to simply go "home" to be with your spouse and children, to recover the core of your vocation: being present to your family.

People feel isolated from God, or even feel that He has abandoned them, because they find it difficult to practice the discipline of listening to His voice in ordinary prayer and ordinary life. Spouses also feel the same sense of isolation from one another if they fail to practice the discipline of listening. If we listen both to one another and to God, however, our identities will be secure in a communion of love. This simple act of listening is pivotal to happiness in prayer and marriage; however, the *process* of becoming a good listener is not simple and may involve the pain of conversion. Nevertheless, we surrender and entrust our desire to become better listeners to Christ Himself, our strength and our power.

Repent

When we fall short of listening to God or beholding His beauty in love, we fail to receive His presence at deeper levels within our heart. Some sins are so grave that we entirely block our capacity for a share in God's own life. These would be the traditional mortal sins, sins where our will and knowledge lead us to choose substantial evil—murder, adultery, fornication, significant theft, etc. For such sins, we are required to go to Confession, therein turning to Christ and asking for His mercy. He is there, in the Sacrament of Reconciliation, ready to forgive us. Just as forgiveness is essential in marriage because it restores intimacy, so forgiveness restores intimacy between ourselves and God, as well; and in the case of mortal sin, repentance and divine forgiveness literally restore us to life, so that we "might have life and have it more abundantly" **(Jn 10:10)**. When we sin, we damage our capacity to adhere to Christ and His will, to receive His love, and to be sent on mission from our worship at the Eucharist. Repentance reconciles us to God. God's grace and love take the initiative and move us to come back to Him. The question is: "Will we respond?"

God moves us to repent and restore our communion with His love through our conscience. This gift of conscience has to be cultivated and nourished only by the best Catholic sources and activities: the Scripture, the *Catechism*, worship, reading the lives of the saints, listening to your spouse challenge or affirm your behavior, following the advice of your pastor or Catholic spiritual director, fellowship with other Catholics and faithful Christians. To nourish the conscience in such a way is to *form it well!* No one is born with a well-formed conscience; we only create such a mind through what we pay attention to.

Until we commit ourselves to listening to such quality sources and participating in such activities, our conscience may only reflect this shallow, passing age (**Rom 12:1-2**). This passing age, or the values of popular Western culture, is transmitted through the media, politics, fashion, entertainment, and financial concerns. Such a conscience does not contain substantial enough nourishment to sustain a Catholic conscience, one that is directing you toward salvation and not simply toward "success" or "acceptance" in and by this age.

If we do not develop a Catholic conscience, we may even miss the fact that our choices are counterproductive to our happiness. Our minds and hearts may simply not recognize that we are unhappy because we choose to live in a world that affirms a cycle of choices that promises more and more of what satisfies less and less. Instead of repenting and no longer choosing such skimpy fare for the human heart, we may mistake restlessness as a sign that we need more affirmation from the culture, more distractions, more activity, instead of choosing to be less "connected" to the present-day society. Ironically, stress, anxiety, and restlessness are the result of connecting deeply to shallow "trends." We receive peace only when we choose to disconnect from our age of distraction and become simple. To be simple is what the human heart really seeks and what God's grace is offering, if we have the courage to repent. To be simple means to put God and your husband or wife first in your life. Simplicity is not barrenness; it is fullness.

One of the most deadly sins in marriage is infidelity, both sexual and emotional. In our relationship with God, we can be unfaithful, as well. Of course, it is unfaithful for a Christian to worship other gods and reject the Trinity. Each and every sin that we commit, however, in some real way, is actually a rejection of God. We always reject God through the act of disobedience to conscience. To disobey the conscience is to disobey the truth as our mind and heart can best judge it. To reject the judgment of the well-formed conscience, as previously noted, is to reject God because God is truth. This is why the simplest definition of sin is: disobedience to a well-formed conscience.[10]

We all need to bring *our own failures* to the Cross of Christ. How does Christ forgive us, and how do we repent of our sins?

How Do We Receive Forgiveness?

"Repent, for the kingdom of heaven is at hand" **(Mt 4:17)**. Christ is aching for us to repent of our sins so that we might receive His life again in fullness. Sin diminishes our capacity to know His love, to feel His consolation. It sets us off on routes that may threaten our return to His love and grace if we allow ourselves to stay away from Him over time. Christ forgives us from the Cross. Right in the midst of His Crucifixion, of His surrender to the Father's love out of love for we who reject Him, He cries out, asking the Father to forgive us all of our sins **(Lk 23:34)**. He forgives us by taking into His heart all of our sins and carrying them mercifully to the Father for healing and reconciliation. Only God can forgive sin because sin is an act that twists and wrenches us away from Him. We cannot find our way back to His love on our own. We are so broken from within our human nature that we can tear away from who we are, but we cannot restore ourselves to our true identity. This true identity, that we are beloved sons and daughters of God, can be bestowed upon us only by God. It cannot be earned or merited or taken or snatched. But due to our broken nature, this true identity can be *given* away by us through our choice to sin. Once we sin, we can receive back the fullness of our dignity only through the Father's act of love in Jesus — God reaching out to us through our own humanity in Jesus of Nazareth. That is how it must be done — God reaching out to us, looking for us, because only He can reconcile what has been torn apart.

To receive forgiveness, then, you must draw close to the mystery of the Cross. But, how? This event is 2,000 years old. As with all things Divine, time is no obstacle, as grace, the very life and love of God, continues to flow from eternity into time and never stops. An historical event may come and go, but the grace, the life of God within that event, is continually offered. Where is this grace offered? Where is it flowing, ever flowing? In the Sacraments. When we participate in the Sacraments with the disposition to be healed and reconciled to God, then we receive all His love and all His life. Repenting is "coming to our senses" **(Lk 15:17)** and choosing again a life of simplicity, a life of communion with the Trinity.

Christ forgives us by and through the power of His identity as God's Son and His actions upon the Cross, actions that make it possible for all humanity to go to the Father as beloved sons and daughters. It is vital that we connect our humanity to this act of God upon the Cross through living a sacramental life. To connect our lives in this way to Christ's own life is what we mean when we say someone has been saved from sin. We become one with Christ through faith, hope, and love; these virtues connect us to the Sacraments, and the Sacraments are *the real presence* of Christ, in the case of the Eucharist, or *the real power of Christ's* merciful and life-giving love, in the case of the six other Sacraments.

How Do We Repent?

"A man had two sons. He came to the first and said, 'Son, go out and work in the vineyard today.' He said in reply, 'I will not,' but afterwards he changed his mind and went" **(Mt 21:28-29)**. You repent by "changing your mind." The Spirit invites you to go beyond the mind you now possess and take on "the mind of Christ" **(Phil 2:5; 1 Cor 2:16)**. You begin the process of taking on the mind of Christ, of having His Spirit guide all of your thoughts, feelings, and desires, by choosing to *live in reality*. If you have chosen sinful actions, *admit it*. Go to Him; recount the actions, and pour them into His merciful heart. We never will be gifted with the Mind of Christ if we do not admit our faults and turn to the Lord for Mercy. Those who do this "turning" to the Lord are never disappointed. He always meets them *in reality*. Stay there to receive His love; stay there to name your faults; stay there despite the pain suffered in knowing the truth about yourself. For, if we leave reality and choose *to hide* our faults, lie about them, or defend ourselves from the pain by blaming others, we never will know the fullness of Divine Mercy.

Only in knowing Divine Mercy will we be restored to a vibrant and developing intimacy with God. If you do not extend forgiveness to and receive forgiveness from your spouse, the communion weakens, unravels, and eventually is so thin that the relationship breaks. As you seek out your spouse to restore weakened or broken bonds when one of you has been unkind or unfaithful, so you are to rush to restore the bond of communion with God. If you can turn back to your spouse and seek his or her face again, then you can certainly seek the face of God, especially since His grace is urging you and supporting you to do so!

So, to summarize: God is calling you to behold Him, listen to Him, and repent when you have weakened or broken your relationship with Him. Here, the virtues and graces of your marital relationship mirror the graces and virtues of your communion with God. The two relationships work interdependently and utilize the same habits to guard your unity with one another and with God through one another. Prayer is a reaching out to receive the presence and love of the merciful God. Marital communication is a reaching out to one another to preserve the bond of love and remain in the presence of one another, remain in reality. Since your wedding, you vowed to enter life together as one, and so your *reality* is your vocation — it is your marriage. Whatever weakens this bond is not real; it is a fantasy, something not worth bothering with! Likewise, God has claimed you as His own, pursued you through life so that He can hold you in reality by and through His love. He desires that you never leave His presence, and anything that takes you from His presence, sin, is to be shunned and fought against. By the design of grace, God is in your spouse and your spouse, in God. God is *for* your marriage and would never lead you away from one another. God is fighting for your bond to remain strong and for both of you to remain in reality with and by the power of His love for you. Keep choosing one another, keep choosing and allowing God to choose you, as well.

Prayer and your loving communication with one another are complementary bonds of communion. If you love your spouse, you can pray; and if you love God and allow God to love you, you can find one another and stay in the presence of one another until death do you part!

chapter 3

Staying in love

"Nothing is more practical than finding God, that is, than falling in love in a quite absolute, final way ... fall in love, stay in love, and it will decide everything."

Marriage of Mary by Domenico Ghirlandaio

Fall in love, stay in love, and it will decide everything

Father Pedro Arrupe, SJ, once said, "Nothing is more practical than finding God, that is, than falling in love in a quite absolute, final way. What you are in love with, what seizes your imagination will affect everything. It will decide what will get you out of bed in the mornings, what you will do with your evenings, how you spend your weekends, what you read, who you know, what breaks your heart, and what amazes you with joy and gratitude. Fall in love, stay in love, and it will decide everything."[11]

Beholding your spouse, listening to your spouse, and forgiving your spouse is the way to *stay in love*. Beholding God in prayer, listening to God in prayer, and repenting when something other than prayer has guided your judgment is the way to *stay in love* with God. The goal for both of these complementary and interpenetrating relationships is to desire, and then welcome, the object of your love, God and spouse, as the reigning presence in your heart. When this happens, you have internalized your beloved and you begin to think *like a spouse*; or in the case of your relationship with God, you begin to think *in prayer*. It has been said that great artists begin to think in music, or think in colors, and so it is with great and holy lovers … they begin to think in love. If you pray and if you internalize your spouse in your heart, you will become one who thinks in love, and to become such a person is to live in reality.

If you stay in love, then all your decisions will flow from that love. That love will be the measure of all the practical things you do every day, as Father Arrupe noted above in his meditation. This, of course, is a very good thing. *You want* your decisions to flow from the core of your marriage and the heart of your love for God. The goal is to have all your decisions flow from your conscious guarding of the bond you have between you as husband and wife, and the bond that Christ has shared with you through His life, Death, and Resurrection. To make decisions from isolation, or from passing moods or emotions like fear or anger or grief, only threatens to pull you into a place of partial truths, partial reality. It is the love and the staying in love that decides your life. Keep choosing the bond of love, and your life will then be one of simple fidelity to your vocation. To live in simple fidelity to your vocation, to *know* who you are, is the greatest of graces and what most people who are suffering complex lives in this age *are hungering to find.*

Appendix A: Questions and Answers

How are we to hear the Spirit speaking in both of us so that we might experience a unified direction to our family life?

There will be times when you will desire two different realities in your marriage. This can range from the trivial (What restaurant do we want to dine at?) to the vital (How many children should we have?). In trivial matters, prayer is not needed, unless the trivial blows up into something bigger, such as the realization that one or the other spouse *always* gets his way when it comes to where to dine, how to spend weekends, or how to understand household roles and chores. Then, if such trivial matters expose a weightier problem in the marriage, you ought to pray and bring Christ directly into the needed forgiveness or sacrifice that is being called for. What has happened here is that the trivial has become the vital, and so praying together becomes essential.

In order for our family to be unified, how do we go about praying and talking our way through differences?

First, remember that God is *the* advocate for your marriage, your emotional and spiritual unity, and your mutual progress in holiness. Even before you begin to pray, know that you have already received an answer from God that echoes all the way down from your wedding day; "Any answer from me to your prayers will be the one that strengthens your vows and your presence to one another." God is all about reconciliation and loving union.

Second, perhaps the vital question you are considering is one about how many children to have and when. Your husband wants to wait until he gets settled in his new job and city, or your wife wishes to begin having children sooner out of love for her vocation to be a mother. You should begin praying through these kinds of vital vocational questions both alone and with one another. Prayer, in other words, is in you and ought not to be just a formal duty when daily night prayers come around. You should be communicating with God throughout the day on such vital decisions that lie before you. Look for signs that He is sending throughout the day. These signs could be confirmations from reading Scripture, counsel from a trusted friend or spiritual adviser, even seemingly random events, such as persons mentioning that you would be great parents, or having your heart moved when you see a dad embrace his baby son. All of these prayer events should be brought to your common prayer as a couple later that day. In fact, these events and the way they are received into your heart constitute the bulk of your prayer together. Sharing these events and their concurrent affective movements with God and your spouse creates the right environment for listening to His will.

What do I mean by affective movements? This expression simply means that we are not "thinking" about God when we pray, but we are giving Him the deepest part of our hearts, the place where deepest thoughts, feelings, and desires dwell. We always are sharing that deep level of our heart with God in prayer because these movements contain our profound longings, longings that, once purified by participation in the sacramental life, can carry God's longings for us, as well.

When I pray, how can I know if I am listening to the Holy Spirit or simply my own thoughts?

We do not want to separate our own self from the Holy Spirit in too radical a way. The Holy Spirit inspires *our own* thoughts and fills them with truths from God. So, it is not a matter of wondering if this voice is mine or His; it is a matter of listening to the truths within my voice and then measuring the contents of the voice with what revelation and Church teaching say about the nature of God. Very few of us ever receive a direct audible utterance from God. His normal path of communication is through the Church, its interpretation of Scripture, and its doctrinal tradition. Most of our "ideas" and any questions we have about obedience toward them are handled on the level of normal doctrinal formation (i.e., Commandments, moral doctrines, etc.). In prayer, also, we may hear a call, a stirred desire to become a missionary, for example. We may need to ask ourselves, "Well, OK, is this God, or do I simply want to leave my home and go very far away?" We normally say it is God after we have noticed peaceful affective movements that deepen our faith, hope, and love and that these movements of attraction do not recede over time. If this is the characteristic of the voice, then go and see a spiritual director who will help you listen ever more deeply to the contents of the voice over time. If the call in the voice facilitates, *makes easier*, your path to holiness, reverences your already established vocation, and respects moral truths of the Church, it is probably God.

Am I wrong to expect consoling, loving feelings from God when I pray?

It is not wrong to expect to be consoled by God when you pray, to feel His love and affection. That expectation and its fulfillment are normal parts of prayer. Of course, good or consoling feelings do not always manifest themselves when we pray.

What happens if I am in a state where I feel sad or separated from God when I pray?

I would say that you should push against these desolate or sad feelings because Christ is always laboring to love us; and love, by its nature, positively moves our affections. Ask Christ to give you the grace to find His love even in times when, on the surface, He feels far away. There are times when desolate, sad feelings will not leave, making them a cross that Jesus invites us to pick up and carry **(Lk 9:23)**. Normally, however, we can receive glimpses of consoling love even in dry times of prayer at the deepest level of our heart, stay there, and keep making acts of faith, hope, and love. In this way, we stay connected to the mystery of God's love for us. Of course, the greatest example of this staying with love, even in the absence of consoling feelings, is Calvary. Here, Christ speaks with, and holds out hope of being heard by, the Father — even when there is no manifestation of consolation. Notice what Jesus does from the Cross, however: *He speaks to the Father.* Jesus' consolation in the pain of the Cross is found in His very speaking to the Father. Pain is not a sign of the Father's rejection or absence. Love can reach through pain. Without this communication in the dark, Jesus would be alone; Jesus speaks to God the Father out of His sadness and pain and, therefore, He is pushing against desolation *even as darkness* is trying to define Him. To push against desolation ("I don't want to pray; I can't pray; I do not feel God; I am alone") is to live out John 1:5: "The light shines in the darkness, and the darkness has not overcome it." Was Jesus feeling consoled upon the Cross? I believe He was because He remained in communication with God the Father. Whereas in hopeless desolation we turn away from communing with God and grasp isolation as our inheritance, Jesus stayed with the Father upon the Cross and, in so choosing, He was consoled even as He was killed.

So, keep praying, even if you do not feel God. Push against the darkness until you see Light, the Light that is always there **(Jn 1:5)**.

Appendix B: A Way of Praying

The Institute for Priestly Formation teaches people how to pray using the acronym ARRR, which stands for *Acknowledge, Relate, Receive, Respond:*

Acknowledge: Prayer is a relationship, a dialogue, between God and man. Since we are called to make a gift of our self,[12] it is necessary first to be in possession of our self, to know our self. To acknowledge is simply to be aware. The awareness that we need for our dialogue with God is specifically the awareness of our *thoughts, feelings,* and *desires*, especially those that directly impact our relationship with God. What am I thinking? How do I feel? What do I desire?

Relate: Simply put, to relate is to *tell Jesus everything!* Nothing is too small to tell Him. To tell Jesus everything is the way to deepest intimacy with God. He already knows who we are, but we need to tell Him. Even if we have told Him the same thing a million times, if we find it in our heart, we need to entrust it to Him again. Some things we take to the Father; others seem to be matters for the Holy Spirit; often we speak to Jesus about the *thoughts, feelings,* and *desires* of our heart; or Mary is constantly ready to receive all that we find in our heart. Thus, as we share the *thoughts, feelings,* and *desires* in our heart with the Trinity or the saints, our love for them grows, and their presence deepens in our heart.

Receive: Our Holy Father, Pope Benedict XVI, explains: "Prayer is pure receptivity to God's grace, love in action, communion with the Spirit who dwells within us, leading us, through Jesus, in the Church, to our heavenly Father. In the power of his Spirit, Jesus is always present in our hearts, quietly waiting for us to be still with Him, to hear His voice, to abide in His love, and to receive 'power from on high,' enabling us to be salt and light for our world."[13] God wants to love us; He is aching to love us. Our stance toward this love is one of vulnerability, openness, and pure receptivity. "God, I desire to be loved by You; I am ready to receive Your love, ready to receive You." God will do this work in us; He will prepare us to receive His love and give to us exactly what we need to be true to our marriage vocation. So, after you relate all your thoughts, feelings, and desires to God, *listen to Him; receive what He longs to give you.*

Respond: We respond to gifts we receive. Our heart's natural *response* to God's love is gratitude. Receiving God impels us — with great ease and simplicity — to *respond.* A *response* flowing from the experience of the love of God is accompanied by joy. In our *response*, we remain in the gift of God, receiving Him always. As we continue to receive His love, He will unleash a new desire: charity toward others. This is the only way we know that we have truly prayed … we can see and feel a new charity in us toward others.

To acknowledge the realities (thoughts, feelings, and desires) in our heart, relate them to the Lord, receive His life in us, and respond in gratitude and generosity is to live the reality of our Baptism. The awareness of what transpires in our hearts throughout the day is the essential foundation for growing in interiority and, consequently, growing in holiness. If we do not enter into relationship with the Lord regarding all that we find in our heart, however, we will rely upon our own strength in striving for holiness and collapse in a heap of despair.

To avoid such a disaster, we simply *tell Jesus everything!* Nothing is too big or small to share with the infinite God Who became an infant. As we converse with the Lord, we will find new experiences in our heart to bring to Him. He will heal pain and sorrow; we will know His love and His life, and He will gently lead us more deeply into His Heart. God is the perfect spouse, the one who loves you in and through death. He *wants* to listen to you.[14]

Endnotes

1 I would like to thank those who read this booklet and made suggested improvements to the text: Valerie Conzett, Jenny Barrett, Gina Switzer, Anthony Lilles, Amy Wulf, Heidi J. Emanuel, Perry Cahall, and Kelsa Brazell.

2 Angelo Cardinal Scola, The *Nuptial Mystery (Ressourcement: Retrieval & Renewal in Catholic Thought)* (Grand Rapids, Michigan: Wm. B. Eerdmans Publishing Co., 2005), 75.

3 There are, of course, situations of brutal emotional and physical abuse for which the moral imperative is simply to find safety away from such abuse. There is, however, what only can be called the "normal" suffering of living with a sinner. This type of activity is not extreme, and when recognized by the offender, she shows signs of real reform and repentance. After forgiveness is bestowed and received, the sinning spouse commits herself or himself to creating an environment of love. To gauge what level of abuse you are in, remember the greatest commandment: You are to love God, others, and self. When abuse is present at the level that demands separation for the sake of safety, one has an almost impossible time loving self, the spouse, or even God.

4 See James Keating, "The Eucharist and the Healing of Affection for Sin" *Emmanuel* (March/April 2007).

5 Your primary spiritual director is your pastor, to whom you will want to recommend Father Scott Traynor's book *The Parish as a School of Prayer: Foundations for the New Evangelization*, (Omaha: IPF Publications, 2013).

6 United States Catholic Conference, *Catechism of the Catholic Church* (CCC) (Washington, DC: USCCB Publishing, 2000), no. 2672. The Holy Spirit, whose anointing permeates our whole being, is the interior Master of Christian prayer. He is the Artisan of the living tradition of prayer. To be sure, there are as many paths of prayer as there are persons who pray, but it is the same Spirit acting in all and with all. It is in the communion of the Holy Spirit that Christian prayer is prayer in the Church.

7 Blessed John Paul II, *Man and Woman He Created Them: A Theology of the Body*, trans. Michael Waldstein (Boston: Pauline Books & Media, 2006), 20:5.

[8] Ruth Burrows, OCD, *Essence of Prayer* (NJ: Paulist Press, 2006), 15.

[9] Documents of Vatican II, *Gaudium et Spes*, no. 24.

[10] In Catholic moral teaching, it is noted that all persons have a duty to form their consciences at a level worthy of human dignity. This means that an exclusive "diet" of sources from only the popular or political culture is not sufficient for the development of a good Catholic conscience. To form a Catholic conscience, a person will include the following in their formation: worship, prayerful reading of the Bible, study of the lives of the saints, the *Catechism*, and consultation with priests or other experts in the spiritual-moral life when important decisions are to be made. If one's conscience is malformed as a result of parents or teachers not exposing a child to the truth, he or she may have lessened culpability in moral matters, until he reaches a reasonable age of moral maturity. Any willful resistance to knowing and living the truth taught by the Church is, itself, a lapse of morality.

[11] Pedro Arrupe, SJ (d. 1991, former Superior General of the Jesuits).

[12] Documents of Vatican II, *Gaudium et Spes*, no. 24.

[13] Pope Benedict XVI, July 20, 2008, 23rd World Youth Day.

[14] Arranged by Jessi Kary, A.O.